5 THINGS YOU MUST DO AFTER A CAR CRASH

STEPHEN SCHOFIELD

WELLS, CALL, CLARK, BENNETT & CLAWSON
620 Great Jones Street, Fairfield, CA 94533
www.WCCBC.com

Ordering Information: Quantity sales. Special discounts are available on quantity purchases by corporations, associations, and others. For details, contact the publisher at the address above.

Printed in the United States of America

DISCLAIMER:
And now, for the obligatory disclaimer (my lawyers made me do it!): Although I hope you find this book contains helpful and valuable information, unless you and I have sat down together, and you have reviewed and signed a retainer agreement for me to represent you, I am not currently your lawyer. If you happen to live in California and would like to meet with me to discuss hiring me to represent you, I would welcome that, but simply by virtue of me writing this book and you reading it, no attorney-client relationship has magically materialized. The advice in this book is intended as general advice only (it's great advice, but it is general - I must admit) and may or may not apply to your specific situation. Every case is unique. Reliance on advice in this book is at your own risk. If you have been in an accident and were injured, you should hire an attorney and rely on that attorney's advice. If you hire me, great! If you hire another attorney, great as well! Either way, this book is merely a general guide. Hire an attorney and rely on that attorney's advice for your specific situation.

TABLE OF CONTENTS

INTRODUCTION

A car accident can be a traumatic experience. I know because I've been in my fair share of them. Immediately your heart starts to pound and your thoughts start to spin with that fight-or-flight adrenaline rush. In that moment and in the moments immediately after the crash, it can be very difficult to gather your thoughts and make clear-headed decisions. The aim of this book is to help you know exactly what to do in the first moments after a crash, and in the following days and weeks so that you can protect your interests.

Thank you for requesting this book. I honestly hope that you will never need the information you'll read in this book because if you do, it means that you've most likely been injured in an accident.

The statistical likelihood of being injured in accidents is not very comforting. Over 3 millions people a year in the United States get injured in an auto accident. Every fourteen seconds someone in this country is injured in a car accident. Thus, no matter how cautious a driver you are, there is a very high probability that the information in this book will directly apply to you someday.

The information in this book is not meant to answer every question or scenario that could come up when one is injured in a car accident. Rather, it describes the essential things you should do after the accident and why you should do them. It is intentionally brief and to the point.

I wish I had read a little book like this before I ever got hurt in a car accident. It could have saved me a lot of trouble. I hope that it can do that for you.

WHY LISTEN TO ME?

I am a practicing personal injury attorney in California. I have handled hundreds of car accident cases throughout the state. I have worked in this field in diverse settings including with a very large personal injury firm, as a solo practitioner, and also in my current role which is with a firm that is just the right size.

I have also had the privilege and challenge of taking numerous cases all the way through a jury trial.

In my experience with many cases, I have certainly seen the bad and the ugly. I have seen clients get taken advantage of by insurance companies (before they came to me). I have had clients die during the representation and have wrapped my arms around their family as they cried. I've had clients come to me talking about the severe depression that the trauma of the accident and injuries and loss of work caused. I've seen attorneys take advantage of their clients and cheat them out of money that rightfully belonged to their clients.

In contrast, I've also seen the good. I've had clients and their families get significant settlements. I've seen clients smile from ear to ear like the weight of the world has been lifted off their shoulders after the jury just ruled in their favor.

I wrote this book to help everyday people know, at the very least, the basics of what they need to understand in order to make smart decisions after being injured in a car accident. This book is not big on the finer details, but it is big on the big picture and on essential action steps.

I hope you come away from reading this book feeling confident that you know the basics of what to do to protect yourself and your loved ones after you've been injured by the careless driving of another.

1

KNOWLEDGE IS POWER

UNDERSTANDING CASE VALUE

I received a desperate call for help one day from a good friend of mine who is a criminal defense lawyer. A family member of his had been in a nasty car wreck and was in the hospital. Knowing that I practice personal injury law, he called me.

Now before I explain why he was desperate and why this call is relevant to this book, I should describe my friend to you a little bit. This friend is a hardcore defender of justice. He's taken dozens of felony cases to jury trial. He knows the ins and outs of criminal law and constitutional law.

This seasoned, passionate, legal warrior called me because his family member was in the hospital with serious injuries after a horrible car wreck, and he was trying to help her with the claim against the insurance company. The problem was that he was completely unsure about how to handle it.

The adjuster told him that the case had a very low settlement value because of this that and the other. He almost settled quick and cheap because he was so persuaded by the insurance adjuster (who's specific goal, I'm sure, was to settle the case quick and cheap). This lawyer who'd been in the trenches in some real legal dogfights was beguiled by the wily adjuster.

Fortunately, I was able to point out to him the flaws in the adjuster's reasoning and point out the tricks that the adjuster was trying to play on him. The adjuster was taking advantage of the fact that my friend did not know the legal landscape he was operating in. I was able to help him realize that his family member's case was very valuable indeed. She had suffered some terrible injuries and she deserved to be compensated for her losses. It was not a case for the adjuster to dump quickly and cheaply.

The reason I bring this example up is that unless dealing with accidents and insurance companies is your life's work, then it is very unlikely that you have any idea what your case is worth, let alone how to ensure that you are compensated accordingly. I don't mean to offend her, and no one should feel bad about this; if my good friend who is a battle-hardened and seasoned criminal defense attorney didn't know these things, how could the average person really be expected to know?

I know from painful personal experience, from long before I made personal injury law my life's work, that insurance companies will do everything they can to settle quickly and cheaply. It is very hard to know what to do after an accident, and it's hard to know what exactly you should be entitled to when a negligent driver comes along and ruins your day, or worse. This is precisely why you should never go it alone!

2

DO AS I SAY, NOT AS I DO

"Knowledge rests not upon truth alone, but upon error also."

Carl Jung

ON A COLD WINTER'S NIGHT

To give you an example of how naive I once was and also to illustrate some key mistakes that are often made, I should tell you about what happened to my family and I one Christmas Eve.

Years ago up in the icy-cold Sierra Nevada Mountains, a drunk driver interrupted an otherwise peaceful and idyllic Christmas Eve when he slammed into the back of my car. Now keep in mind, this all happened long before I became a personal injury lawyer, and I was as clueless as they come about how to deal with this kind of situation. I share the following story in order to point out the mistakes I made in the way I reacted and responded to being injured in an accident.

Hopefully, you can learn from my mistakes and learn the right way to handle this kind of situation if, heaven forbid, you happen to suffer the misfortune of being struck by a negligent driver. Perhaps mixing a little of what I have learned in my years of practice as a personal
injury attorney with the following tale from my own life will help you more easily remember the critical actions to take if you find yourself in a similar position.

Okay. On with the story.

I was driving a large SUV, and I had my wife, our two daughters, and my nephew in the car. My youngest was just a baby, and she was securely buckled (thank goodness) in a rear-facing car seat at the time. She was only about two months old. We were up in the mountains visiting my parents and siblings. It was freezing cold and there was snow on the ground, but the skies were clear, and the roads were dry and ice-free. We had just driven down the street to pick up extra hot cocoa packets to enhance the Christmas cheer.

We were driving back to my parents' house, and we stopped at a stop sign literally just a block away from my parents' house. Suddenly it felt like thunder clapped directly on top of our car. In the hazy moment that followed I even wondered if we had just been struck by lightning. I immediately heard my daughter crying. Only then did it occur to me that we had been rear-ended.

I quickly checked on my wife who was sitting next to me up front. Fortunately, she was okay, just shaken up. The kids, and yes, even the baby, seemed to be okay. I got out of the car and walked around back to see what had happened.

The front end of the car that hit us looked like an upside down steel taco. Smoke and steam were pouring out both ends. My car looked more or less alright, as the other car had sort of slid under it. The driver sheepishly came up to me and apologized for wrecking my car. I don't remember whether or not he even noticed that there were kids inside. He didn't ask if we were okay.

I stepped aside to call my dad to ask him to come out and give us a hand with the situation. After all, we were about 20 yards from his house. I turned back around to talk with the guy who just smashed us; I was planning to exchange insurance information so his insurance company could repair my car. Low and behold, the man was gone. I scanned the vicinity in the cold and dark, my heart was still pounding with adrenaline. Then I saw the man slinking away down an adjacent street with no streetlights. I ran over to him and stood in front of him, cutting him off.

Just then my dad had also arrived, so we had the guy outnumbered. If I can recall correctly, I think the guy tried to make up some story just then about how he was going somewhere to make a phone call, and then he'd come right back. My dad and I said, "no way pal," and kindly escorted him back to the smoking pile of twisted metal.

The cops arrived the minute we got back to the scene. I'm not sure who called them. We exchanged info and gave statements to the police officers. The officers informed me that the man was drunk driving.

Then we went our separate ways. For the other driver that meant off to jail (sorry, not sorry). For us, that meant home to the fire, hot cider, and Christmas carols.

However, that drunkard really smacked into us pretty hard, and we each took a pretty decent jolt in the accident. We were all a little sore. We thought about going to the ER, but hey, we weren't bleeding; we could walk, and it was Christmas Eve for crying out loud. Who wants to spend their Christmas Eve in the ER? Not us, we decided. Besides, we figured ER visits were so expensive, and we just couldn't afford it. Especially right after Christmas.

Over the next couple of days, I felt increasingly sore. I did my best to shake it off with some Tylenol and Advil, but the pain still managed to make my life difficult.

Meanwhile, the insurance adjuster from the other driver's insurance company was calling me. He asked me the first day after the accident if everyone was okay if anyone was injured. I told him I wasn't sure everyone was okay if anyone was injured. I told him I wasn't sure just yet, but that probably not and that no one was seeking any medical treatment.

A couple days later he called and offered a thousand dollars to each person in the car. I was so naive that I felt like this was some kind of lucky windfall, and I excitedly accepted the offer. I signed the release, which he emailed to me right away, and I got a check in the mail within a couple of days. I thought I had really scored!

Things changed, however, when I got back to work after the Christmas break. That's when the pain really started to get to me. Sitting at my desk hour after hour, my back, especially my lower back, was in pain almost constantly. It made it difficult to concentrate.

I tried stretching, walking around, and Advil. It all helped a little, but the pain persisted still for at least a couple of months. I never did end up going to the doctor. I had lame insurance at the time, and I just didn't want to have more bills to pay. Also, I grew up playing competitive sports like wrestling and football, so "playing through the pain" was kind of hardwired into my system.

THE RIPPLE EFFECTS

In time, my symptoms did resolve, but a few things just didn't sit right with me. For one, my lovely Christmas Eve celebration got messed up! That wasn't my fault, nor my daughters', nor my wife's. It was that stupid drunk driver who spinelessly tried to slink off into the night and avoid responsibility for his stupidity. One minute we were all having a great time, visions of sugar plums dancing in our heads and all that, then wham! Things got thrown off track. We spent the rest of that night sort of adjusting back to reality and feeling really tired.

Another thing that nagged at me was that over the next few days when we should have just been chilling, enjoying the Christmas break
and the days off of work, we ended up spending hours dealing with a messed up car. Driving it to the body shop, waiting for it to get fixed,
and dealing with the insurance companies, rental car companies, etc. It was a tremendous pain in the neck (no pun intended). Once again, it was not my fault. It was that dummy that hit us fault, yet we were paying the price. It felt so unfair.

On top of those two nagging annoyances and inconveniences, I was in pain! I had just started a new job, and I had to sit in that desk all day with that back pain taking up my energy and attention that was already stretched thin due to adjusting to a new job. My back hurt, and that was also not my fault. On top of all this, there were my daughters, my wife, and my nephew, that all dealt with the stress, disappointment, and physical pain of the ordeal.

Lucky for us, our injuries were minor. After having spent years as a personal injury attorney since then, I have seen some unspeakably awful things happen to my clients also through no fault of their own. I mean truly terrible tragedies that make my little "ordeal" seem like a walk in the park. I by no means want to make it out like my suffering was in any way comparable to those situations or perhaps something that you may have suffered yourself or that someone close to you may have suffered.

I also know, however, that many of the readers of this book have been in similar situations as I was, i.e., not tragic or major - but still rotten, and have been frustrated in much the same way as I was.

In the rest of this book, I will walk you through some of the mistakes I made in dealing with the Christmas Eve crash and show you the right way to respond and react if something like this happens to you. I will give you tools to deal with insurance companies and help you understand your rights and the different types of compensation you may be entitled to.

3

SOMEBODY CALL 911!

Fortunately for me, the police showed up on their own to my Christmas Eve accident scene. Had they not, I'm not sure I would have had the wherewithal at the moment to call them, and the other driver probably would have been able to sneak off at some point when I was distracted doing something else, like calming a screaming baby.

I'm not sure why they showed up - probably because it was a small town and we were two out of the twelve or so cars that were even on the road at that time. I am glad the police did show up. They were able to interview everyone involved, including witnesses. They discovered the other guy was drunk, and they took him away. They took detailed photos to document all aspects of the property damage.

BUT I DON'T HAVE TIME!

It is critically important to call the police after an accident. It can seem like a low priority. The timing is always bad. It can add on quite a bit of extra delay to an already inconvenient predicament. Anytime we get in an accident it is the worst possible time for it to happen. We might be on our way to work, or taking the kids to a performance, or any number of more important things. We lead busy lives these days. But in the vast majority of situations, it is worth your time to call the police and wait for their arrival.

Sometimes the police won't come. Sometimes they will come but will only take a cursory look at the situation, make sure that insurance info is exchanged, then get out of there. But other times they will come and make thorough written reports. They will interview everyone around, everyone that was involved, get ambulances to the scene, and take pictures and sometimes video.

I've had clients come in and tell me that at the scene of the accident the other driver admitted it was their fault and was very apologetic. Then I talk to the adjuster on the other side, and suddenly they're denying liability because of the description they got from the other driver, their insured.

That's why I say call the police. The police will interview the other driver at the scene, where there is physical evidence and they have to speak face to face. It's much harder for the other driver to get away with a made up story then.

Also, sometimes getting a witness's statement at the scene is the only place you are going to be able to get it. People disappear. The police officer can get that statement and he or she will put it in his report along with the witness's name, address, and phone number. When liability and damages are all clearly laid out in a police report, that other driver may still try a bit of revisionist history with his insurance company, but it's just not going to work.

If it's a possible DUI case, the police can also collect the evidence needed to prove the other driver was driving under the influence.

Merely telling the adjuster or a jury that you thought the other driver smelled like booze is not going to be enough - most of the time. However, if the police sniff it out at the scene, then do a breath test, then do field sobriety tests, then a blood test and the other driver is later convicted for DUI, well . . . that's pretty much a done deal. It would be practically indisputable at that point. Without the police though, your mere suspicion that the other driver was DUI is pretty flimsy.

Sure there is a chance the police might show up and basically do nothing, act like you're wasting their time, and then leave, but who cares. It's still the best practice. Most of the time they will show up and be helpful and provide you with critical assistance at the moment.

4

A PICTURE IS WORTH
A THOUSAND WORDS

"Photography is the story I fail to put into words."

Destin Sparks

At the time of the Christmas Eve incident, I failed to take any pictures whatsoever. I didn't get pictures of either vehicle, of the other driver, or of anything else for that matter. Now I don't recall exactly whether or not I even had a smartphone yet or not. It's been a while. This accident may have predated the smartphone era. If that's true, then I'm letting myself off the hook.

Nowadays, however, unless you are seriously injured, and I mean seriously injured, like you can't lift your arm to snap a picture with your phone or you might die, there is no excuse for not taking pictures as soon as possible at the scene of the accident.

Pictures are important, and I'll tell you why. If it's not documented, it didn't happen. Even if you think you're okay, you think you're not injured, and that you're not going to be filing an injury claim, you still need to document as much detail about the accident as you can. You may wake up the next morning, or a couple of days later, with neck and back pain.

If you didn't take pictures, there are certain things that will become more difficult (sometimes impossible) to prove, especially if the other driver starts being dishonest with the insurance companies and trying to turn the tables on you (which does happen).

You need to take pictures of both cars from as many angles as possible. If the cars are still where they came to rest after the accident, take pictures of the overall layout of the crash. You need to take pictures of the other driver, his or her driver's license and insurance docs, and street signs.

If you are frazzled, dazed, and confused by all the chaos that often ensues after an accident, please just try to remember to at least get a good shot of the damage to both cars, and the license and insurance information of the other driver.

THE SLIPPERY TORTFEASOR

I represented a client once who was injured by another driver. He got out and they talked. He told her he was going to go get her some ice real quick for her injury, then he drove off and just never came back. No one got a picture of his car or driver's license, so there was no way to hold him responsible.

BRING THE PAIN TO LIFE

If you're wondering why it is so critical to document the property damage with photos, I'll put it another way: pictures bring your pain to life. If it turns out you're injured (which you may know right away or may not realize until later) and you pursue a claim with the insurance company it can be tremendously helpful to have pictures to show the insurance adjuster, or ultimately if it comes down to it, the jury.

It is one thing to tell an adjuster or jury that the car was dented up real bad and the window was smashed and the repair estimate was $11,000. It is quite another for the adjuster or the jury to be looking at dozens of HD color photos of an accordioned car hood, a crumpled door, or whatever the case may be.

It's also important that the pictures be of both cars. Sometimes the damage to one car does not appear to be severe, while the other car is mangled beyond recognition.

The point is that the adjuster and ultimately a jury will use the pictures to gauge the severity of the impact. If the cars are bashed up, and the adjuster or jury is looking at dozens of detailed, high-quality photos, or even video of the damage, your case value is going up. Vivid photos help make the crash real and bring it to life in a way that mere words and dollar amounts of repair estimates can never do.

Whether we like it or not, juries, and of course, adjusters, are skeptical when it comes to someone saying they were injured in an accident. Having quality, graphic, proof of the damage and severity of the impact of the collision helps curb that skepticism.

5

DON'T BE A HERO

"I've separated my shoulder and my collarbone; I've messed up my knee a million times. I've broken my foot in several places. I've broken my toe a bunch, broken my nose a couple of times, and had a bunch of other annoying little injuries, like turf toe and arthritis and tendonitis. It's part of the game."

> Ronda Rousey
> UFC Fighter

"I take great pride in going out there and playing through the pain."

> David Wright
> Major League Baseball Player

You don't have to be a hero after you've been in an accident. Real life is not a game. It's not a Marvel superhero movie, the Super Bowl, or the

UFC. If you're hurt, it's important to you and those around you that you take time out and focus on getting the help you need from professionals in order to get better and be the best version of yourself you can be.

As I told you earlier, my family and I didn't go to the ER that night because, well, it was Christmas Eve. Yes, I was worried about my health and that of my family, but hey, we were just a little sore. We were dazed and fatigued, but all we wanted was to just relax by the fire and enjoy what was left of our already-tarnished Christmas Eve. Who could blame us? Well, an insurance adjuster for one! Ha!

In order to get adequate compensation for an injury, you have to do more than just simply SAY you are hurt. Whether your injury is serious and painful and awful, or whether it's more just annoying and a bother, you will not get much from an insurance company for it unless you can prove it. Your honest word that you were injured and you suffered pain is a form of legitimate proof, it's testimony; however, it may not be enough. It can be very persuasive, but in a vacuum and out of context, with no supporting medical records, it can fall flat. The doctor holds the key to documenting your injury.

Your testimony or say-so along with medical records, doctors notes, medical bills, X Rays, etc., is one billion times more persuasive and credible than just your own testimony. Now I am by no means advocating that you go get medical treatment if you are not in fact injured. But if you have pain, and you don't get treatment, the insurance adjuster is going to hear you crying and asking for some compensation, and he will laugh in your face. The adjuster will not care and will not give you any kind of real settlement money unless you have been seeing the doctor to get help with your injury and your pain. It is critical that you get treatment and that you do not delay getting it.

HOW SOON SHOULD YOU GET TREATMENT?

In general, it is wise to avoid gaps in treatment. If you go a long time after the crash without seeing a doctor, insurance defense attorneys would argue that you must not really have been in much pain and therefore did not suffer damages. So if you're the kind of person (like me) that tends to "play through the pain," the time after a car accident is definitely not the time to do it.

Now there may be differences of opinion on this point, but my feeling is that if you've been in a wreck where either your car, the other

driver's car, or both are mangled, whether you're in serious pain or not, you should go get checked out by a doctor right away. Having your body knocked around that hard, with that much force, can really do a number.

You also have high levels of adrenaline pumping through your veins right after an accident because of the shock of it all. This means that you may not necessarily feel the pain right away. It's just how our bodies are wired. So I would advocate going to the ER right away, or at the very least getting to an urgent care clinic the same day.

If you are already in extreme pain immediately after the accident, this may seem obvious, but I've had many, many clients who were in extreme pain that just went straight home to ice it up and try to sleep it off in the hopes that they'd magically feel better in the morning. What happens most of the time in that situation is that they end up waking up feeling worse, and to add insult to injury (bad pun - sorry), they just significantly decreased the value of their claim by not getting medical treatment immediately.

Typically it is best, both for your health and well-being and for ensuring you get just compensation for your troubles, to go immediately to get medical treatment. This is true, in my opinion, whether you are hurt bad, or on the other hand, whether you are not sure but from the looks of your car you feel like you should be hurt bad (unfortunately you'll probably be feeling it in the next day or two).

WHAT ABOUT THE COST?

The simple truth here is hard for some people to accept, but the reality is that in the vast majority of cases you are not going to have to pay for medical treatment. Of course, there are exceptions to every rule (talk to a lawyer), but as a general principle, the insurance company of the dummy who hit you is going to pay for it. So many people who are hurt in accidents decline that ambulance ride the police officer at the scene is encouraging them to take, and further, they skip the visit to the ER altogether, simply because they want to avoid the cost. This is typically unnecessary.

Ever hear the phrase "penny-wise and pound-foolish?" That expression could not be more appropriate for this situation. By skipping the ambulance ride or the ER visit, you decrease the value of your claim, and worse, severe injuries may go undiscovered.

You'll get a bill from the ambulance company and from the ER or urgent care, but ultimately that bill will be made part of the demand package that your personal injury lawyer sends to the insurance company. If the ER or the ambulance company starts to get nervous and is wondering why you are not paying your bill, your personal injury lawyer will call them and tell them to chill - they will get their money.

So the takeaway is: get to the ER or urgent care the same day of your accident. You will be glad you did. Err on the side of caution. Your health is your most valuable asset at the end of the day.

6

KNOW YOUR ENEMY

"If you know the enemy and know yourself, you need not fear the result of a hundred battles. If you know yourself but not the enemy, for every victory gained you will also suffer a defeat. If you know neither the enemy nor yourself, you will succumb in every battle."

Sun Tzu
The Art of War

Boy oh boy! I could really get going on this topic. I'll do my best to keep myself within acceptable norms of civilized society.

Let's get a few things straight. First of all, the insurance adjuster is not your friend. They talk a good game, for sure. It may seem like they are really helping you out and that they "get" you. Don't be a sucker!

They are wolves in sheeps' clothing. Their job is to save the insurance company money. They accomplish that job by making sure you get as little money as possible. They take advantage of the fact that you are in a vulnerable state.

After an accident, people are stressed; they're scrambling. Their transportation is down. They need to figure out how they are going to get around - how they're going to get to work, take the kids to school, etc. They're in physical pain from getting their body knocked around. They may be experiencing emotional trauma such as PTSD or depression. Also, most of us are running around broke half the time, so when an accident like this happens the financial stress can really reach a boiling point.

After an accident, people are looking for help from someone. They know by instinct that they need to contact insurance to report the accident and file a claim. So along comes the friendly adjuster (licking his or her chops).

Now is the point where most accident victims start spilling their guts. They found someone to talk to. With every word that comes out of their mouth at this point, there is an incredibly high likelihood that they are hurting their claim.

It's not their fault any more than it is a gazelle's fault when they are getting eaten by a lion on the savannah, but it is true. The adjuster is taking note, or sometimes recording the conversation. The adjuster is looking for any little detail that may be used to reduce the value of the claim.

In the immediate aftermath of an accident, maybe when you haven't taken stock of every part of your body that is hurting you, the adjuster may ask you about your pain levels and areas of pain. You know your back hurts really bad, but you forget to mention the nagging pain in your knee. Later, when it turns out that that nagging pain in your knee (that you failed to mention to the adjuster) required months of physical therapy to stop hurting you, the insurance company refuses to pay the physical therapy bills because you stated that you did not have pain to your knee in that early conversation, so, therefore, it must have happened later, and therefore, they are not on the hook for it.

That's just one example of the many, many ways they will ensnare you when you start talking. In my Christmas Eve case, I told the adjuster that we were all okay, shaken up, but okay. I told them we were a little sore and might go to the doctor, but that we probably wouldn't need to and that I thought we'd be okay. This was right after the accident. You can imagine what that simple conversation did to my case.

I had a client who came into my office after he was rear-ended on the freeway on his way home from work. He was in incredible pain. He winced as he sat in front of me because his back hurt so bad just sitting there
.

He came in to see me because he had spoken with the adjuster and she had offered him $250.00 to settle. She offered him that on the day of the accident. She even offered to have it direct deposited into his checking account that day. $250.00!

This was a slap in the face to a man that supports a wife and three kids with his construction job which he now may not be able to get back to for months. But, he was tempted to take it in that moment of confusion and weakness and vulnerability after the accident because of the adjuster's beguiling words.

PLEAD THE FIFTH

In a previous phase of my career, I practiced private criminal defense. In that line of work, the watch cry is, "DON'T TALK TO THE POLICE!"

The founding fathers knew that opening your mouth at certain times and places to certain people could get you into serious trouble. That is why we have the Fifth Amendment to the U.S. Constitution.

We have the right to remain silent when being interrogated by the police. While the adjuster is clearly not a police officer or in any way affiliated with law enforcement, and our liberty is not on the line when we're pursuing an accident and injury claim, the same principle applies. Whatever you say to the adjuster can and will be held against you in court, in mediation, and even in informal settlement negotiations.

It's not codified in the Constitution, but we do have a right to remain silent when it comes to the other driver's insurance adjuster. In some situations, you do have to talk to your own insurance company's adjuster about the accident, your injuries, and your treatment, but your attorney can advise you in that regard.

With the at-fault driver's insurance company, however, you definitely do not ever have to talk to that adjuster, and you definitely should not discuss the accident, your injuries, or your medical treatment with them, EVER . . . unless your attorney advises you to do so, which would be exceedingly rare.

ISN'T MY OWN COMPANY'S ADJUSTER MY FRIEND?

No. Not really.

You must always think about any adjuster as an adverse adjuster, as in someone who has an interest that is not in line with yours. As I said before, their job is to save their company's money, not your money. Doing their job almost always comes at your expense.

At first, it may seem that your insurance company would naturally be on your side, but what if it turns out that the other driver didn't have insurance? Or what if the other driver didn't have enough insurance to cover your damages? If you have uninsured motorist coverage, then your claim is going to be against your own insurance company and an adversarial relationship is then in place.

Then it's you and against your own insurer. They're on one side, the side that doesn't want to give you money and will look for any reason to justify lowering the value of your claim. You're on the other side - the side that's been injured and wronged through no fault of your own - the side that needs the money in order to be made whole and for justice to prevail.

So the point here is, be careful, and try to keep your conversation only on the property damage, car repair, car rental, and facts of the accident. Don't talk to any adjuster about your injuries or pain levels.

7

LAWYER UP!

"He who represents himself has a fool for a client."

Abraham Lincoln

The next big mistake I made after the Christmas Eve crash was that I did not hire an attorney to represent me and handle my case. Not only did the founding fathers of this country understand the importance of keeping one's trap shut, but they also understood the importance of having someone else do the talking for you. The point is that when there is a lot at stake, we often need the help of an experienced professional.

Real talk here: sometimes we just need a pro. It doesn't mean we're dumb or incapable. It's just the smart move. When our health, our wealth, or our liberty is at stake, we need pros. After an accident, two of those three, namely health and wealth, are at stake.

THE PROBLEM OF VALUE

Just like we discussed at the beginning of this book, it is very hard for anyone to know the value of his or her case. When the adjuster comes along with a meager settlement offer, how is one to know whether or not the offer is reasonable or not, having no context or frame of reference. To clarify this particular situation allow me to use a (hopefully) helpful analogy.

Imagine if you will that you were dropped into a foreign country where you didn't speak the language. In that country, they have their own currency, but you have no idea of the relative exchange value for U.S. Dollars. You decide you are going to buy a car (I know it may seem odd that buying a car would be the first thing you'd do if you were dumped in some mystery country but hey, we're just pretending here so please play along). So you go to a car lot and none of the cars have prices posted on them. You see the car you want, and the salesman approaches you and says in broken English, "five thousand."

So now you have some information. That car costs 5,000. Presumably that 5,000 is in this foreign country's currency. So you now know that the car you want is going to cost 5,000. Sounds like a good deal right? You really need a car, and this guy is ready to sell you one right now. Problem solved. Done deal.

But wait . . . there's just one small issue. You don't know what the other cars are being sold for. You don't know what that car you want is worth, relative to the others. But hey, this car salesman you just met probably has your best interests in mind right? He is very friendly. He wouldn't try to take advantage of your lack of understanding of the market.

You get the idea, i.e., Foreign Car Salesman = Insurance Adjuster ;-) How can you know if the insurance adjuster is offering you what your case is worth? It is certainly not their job to make sure you get a fair settlement. They're just like that stranger selling you a used car. His job is to make money for the car lot. The insurance adjuster's job is to make money for the insurance company. That means their interests are diametrically opposed to yours.

It sure would be nice if there was someone on your side who knew what cases were worth and could help you know if you were getting a raw deal or not. In our foreign car lot example wouldn't it be nice if you had a friend with you on that lot who spoke the language, who was a local instead of a foreigner, and who had made a career out of helping people get good deals?

Enter, the personal injury lawyer. If you hire a lawyer to represent you after an accident, that lawyer has an ethical duty to zealously advocate for your interests and to fight hard to make sure you get the most money possible to cover your damages.

Also, if you choose a lawyer that specifically practices personal injury and motor vehicle accident law, then you can know that that lawyer deals with adjusters and settlements in cases very similar to yours every single day. You can bet that that lawyer will have a darn good sense as to whether or not you are getting a fair offer or not. If the adjuster is trying to get away with one and take you for a sucker, the lawyer will put a stop to that.

LAWYER AS NEGOTIATOR

While evaluating cases is a critical skill your lawyer will bring to the table, there is more to it than just that. Yes, the personal injury lawyer knows how to evaluate offers for fairness and keeps the adjuster honest, but a good personal injury lawyer is also a skilled negotiator. Ideally, he or she will have honed his or her negotiating skills in countless courtrooms, judges' chambers, hallways, and conference tables throughout your state.

A very wise, old lawyer taught me at the beginning of my career to treating every case as if it is going to trial. This is the ultimate way to have the most power possible in negotiations. When a lawyer is prepared to take a case to trial and knows the case in and out, the adjuster can sense that that lawyer is "for real." The adjuster is then far more likely to make "for real" offers.

That being said, the cases that actually do wind up in a trial are few and far between. More often than not, it serves all parties' best interest to reach a fair settlement. However, a fair settlement is always based on the credible threat of a lawsuit and a trial. The more credible the threat, the fairer the settlement. If that threat is hollow, the offers will show it. So the battle-tested trial lawyer brings more clout to the bargaining table, and the offers tend to go up.

CUTTING THROUGH RED TAPE

To recap, by retaining a lawyer your ability to evaluate the fairness of an offer instantly becomes greatly enhanced. Your power at the negotiating table also gets a huge instant boost. There's also another way a lawyer can be of great help. The lawyer and his staff save you from having to deal with the endless red tape, phone calls, forms, and letters that come with dealing with insurance companies. By being able to leave the legal and bureaucratic headaches to the law office, the injured party can focus on healing and getting his or her life back on track. There is enough to worry about after an accident without having to deal with all the garbage that insurance companies try to put you through.

WHAT ABOUT LAWYER FEES?

Now at this point, you may be thinking to yourself, "Yeah I get it, a lawyer is helpful because x,y, and z, and so on and so on, but a lawyer has got to get paid right? I don't have that kind of money (or, I don't want to have to share my settlement)." If that is anything like what you are thinking, then you are not alone. I was thinking the same sort of thing after my Christmas Eve accident.

What you need to understand is that personal injury lawyers only get paid if you get paid. That is, their fee is a contingency fee. If they get you a good settlement or the jury awards you money, the lawyer will get paid from that money. You don't have to pay out of pocket. Also, the lawyer will front all the costs and do all the work.

While the lawyer does ultimately get paid a fee out of the settlement, studies have shown that when a lawyer is representing a victim, the settlements are on average three times greater than if the victim has no lawyer. This statistic was from a recent study by the Insurance Research Council (IRC). The IRC is a non-profit founded in 1977.

The organization actually receives its support from the insurance companies, so it is by no means a shill for the personal injury bar. The research is legitimate. Lawyers help victims get more money. By the

IRC's study, "more" means three times more than victims that don't have attorneys.

So yes, the lawyer gets paid, but so do you, and you always get more* than the attorney. You no longer have to put up with the red tape and rigamarole, and you are likely to end up with even more money at the end of the day.

It's up to you whether or not you hire a lawyer to help you. Obviously, I have some bias because I am a personal injury lawyer. However, I can honestly tell you that I wish that I had hired a lawyer to help me after I got rear-ended on that Christmas Eve.

*SIDE NOTE: If you ever hear of a personal injury attorney that is willing to take a fee that's larger than what their client is actually getting from a settlement or jury award, that is a lawyer to be avoided. Unfortunately, it happens all the time. I've seen them do it. It's not okay with me.

8

CONCLUSION

To echo my opening remarks to this book, I sure hope you never end up needing the information that you've read here. Now that you've read it, however, I hope that you can retain it so that you can act decisively and confidently if you are ever injured by someone else's bad driving. I hope you'll be able to protect yourself in the aftermath by remembering these five action steps.

Take pictures of everything - even video if you can. At a minimum get pictures of the damage to all vehicles involved, the other car's license plate, the other driver's insurance info and driver's license. Once those bases are covered, see if you can get pictures of street signs, landmarks, skid marks, the positioning of vehicles, witnesses, etc.

Call the police. Maybe they'll help, maybe they won't, but they probably will. They definitely won't if you don't call.

Get medical treatment. The sooner the better. In most instances, I would advise ER or at least urgent care the same day. Get in that ambulance if it's bad. Don't be a hero!

Don't talk to that adjuster. Remember they are not your friend. Their job is to save the insurance company's money. That usually means making sure you get as little of it as possible. It's okay to talk to them about property damage or to talk to them if your lawyer says to do so. Other than that, mum's the word.

Get a lawyer. A good personal injury lawyer can make a world of difference for you after an accident. He or she will help you get top dollar for your claim, even if it means taking it all the way to the jury (rare, but it can be necessary). Also, he or she will save you from a nightmarish amount of red tape and hassle.

Again, thank you for taking the time to read this book. Please pass it along to someone else who may need it.

Feel free to contact me if you need me. My contact info can be found in the "About the Author" section that follows.

Cheers,

Stephen Schofield

ABOUT THE AUTHOR

Stephen Schofield is happily married and lives with his wife and three daughters in Northern California. He is a fluent Spanish speaker.

Stephen currently works for the personal injury law firm of Wells, Call, Clark, Bennett & Clawson with offices spread throughout Northern California.

Prior to his current position, he spent a number of years as a private criminal defense trial lawyer in Sacramento and surrounding counties. He was honored by the National Trial Lawyers in 2017 when they named him as one of the top 40 trial lawyers in California under the age of 40.

Stephen graduated from the William S. Boyd School of Law at the University of Nevada, Las Vegas in 2010. While in law school he was invited onto the staff of the school's law review, The Nevada Law Journal. He also volunteered with a local non-profit legal aid clinic, assisting Spanish-speakers with legal documents.

After law school, Stephen accepted an offer for a judicial clerkship in the First Judicial District of Nevada, where he worked for over a year. After passing the California bar exam on his first attempt and obtaining his license to practice law, Stephen began working for a large California personal injury firm in the Bay Area where he learned many valuable lessons that he uses in his current practice.

Contact Information:

WELLS, CALL, CLARK, BENNETT & CLAWSON
Phone: (800) 847-8765
Email: stephen@wccbc.com
www.WCCBC.com

www.ingramcontent.com/pod-product-compliance
Lightning Source LLC
Chambersburg PA
CBHW020956180526
45163CB00006B/2389